4 Times Table

Learn the 4 times table so that you can reme

Colour the number 4 and the

GW00492882

Learn

1	x 4	=	**4**
2	x 4	=	**8**
3	x 4	=	**12**
4	x 4	=	**16**
5	x 4	=	**20**
6	x 4	=	**24**
7	x 4	=	**28**
8	x 4	=	**32**
9	x 4	=	**36**
10	x 4	=	**40**

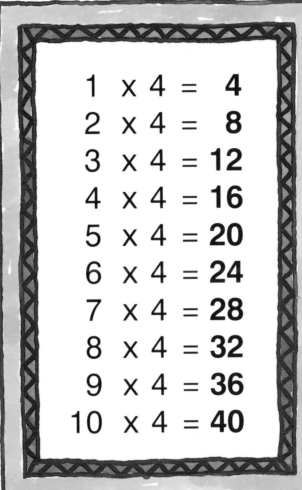

Do these sums.

$2 + 2 =$ $\qquad$ $6 - 2 =$

$1 + 3 =$ $\qquad$ $8 - 4 =$

5 Times Table

Learn the 5 times table so that you can remember it from 1 to 10.
Colour the number 5 and the butterflies.

Learn

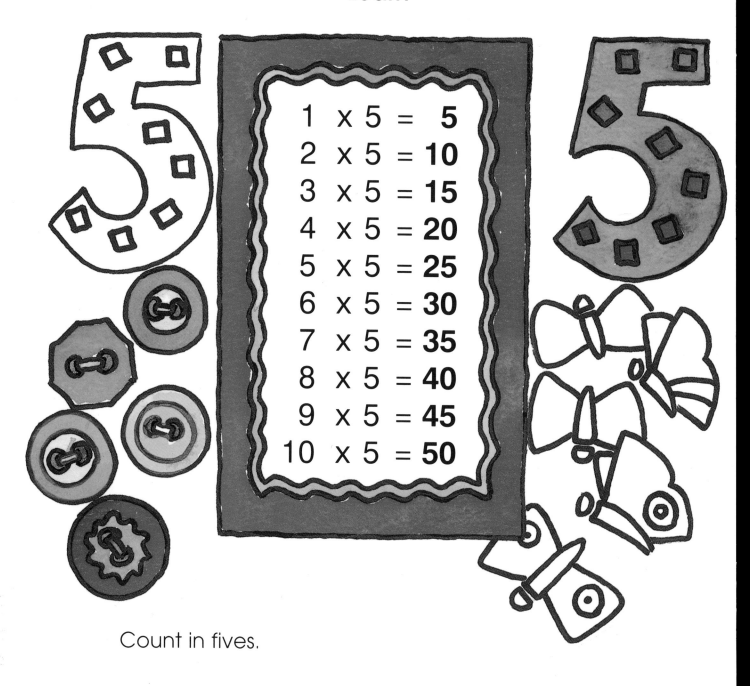

1	x 5 =	**5**
2	x 5 =	**10**
3	x 5 =	**15**
4	x 5 =	**20**
5	x 5 =	**25**
6	x 5 =	**30**
7	x 5 =	**35**
8	x 5 =	**40**
9	x 5 =	**45**
10	x 5 =	**50**

Count in fives.

5   10   ☐   20

☐   30   35   ☐

6 Times Table

Learn the 6 times table so that you can remember it from 1 to 10.
Colour the number 6 and the balls.

Learn

1	x 6	=	6
2	x 6	=	12
3	x 6	=	18
4	x 6	=	24
5	x 6	=	30
6	x 6	=	36
7	x 6	=	42
8	x 6	=	48
9	x 6	=	54
10	x 6	=	60

Write the answers in the boxes.

How many ducks are on this page?

How many balls?

Add the ducks and the balls together.

7 Times Table

Learn the 7 times table so that you can remember it from 1 to 10.
Colour the number 7 and the aeroplanes.

Learn

1	x 7	=	7
2	x 7	=	14
3	x 7	=	21
4	x 7	=	28
5	x 7	=	35
6	x 7	=	42
7	x 7	=	49
8	x 7	=	56
9	x 7	=	63
10	x 7	=	70

Do these exercises.

4 x 7 = ⎯⎯⎯⎯⎯⎯⎯   ⎯⎯ x 7 = 21 ⎯⎯⎯⎯⎯

8 x 7 = ⎯⎯⎯⎯⎯⎯⎯   6 x 7 = ⎯⎯⎯⎯⎯⎯⎯

8 Times Table

Learn the 8 times table so that you can remember it from 1 to 10.
Colour the number 8 and the cups.

Learn

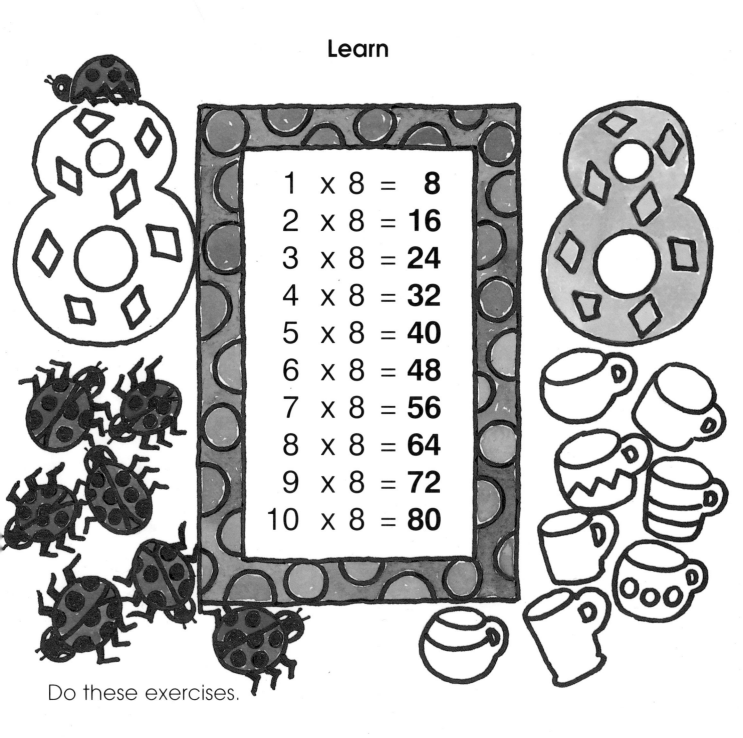

1	x 8	=	**8**
2	x 8	=	**16**
3	x 8	=	**24**
4	x 8	=	**32**
5	x 8	=	**40**
6	x 8	=	**48**
7	x 8	=	**56**
8	x 8	=	**64**
9	x 8	=	**72**
10	x 8	=	**80**

Do these exercises.

4 x 2 =   16 ÷ 2 =

5 + 3 =   18 − 10 =

9 Times Table

Learn the 9 times table so that you can remember it from 1 to 10.
Colour the number 9 and the bows.

Learn

1	x 9 =	**9**
2	x 9 =	**18**
3	x 9 =	**27**
4	x 9 =	**36**
5	x 9 =	**45**
6	x 9 =	**54**
7	x 9 =	**63**
8	x 9 =	**72**
9	x 9 =	**81**
10	x 9 =	**90**

Do these exercises.

___ x 9 = 9   6 x 9 = ___

3 x ___ = 27   ___ x 9 = 90

10 Times Table

Learn the 10 times table so that you can remember it from 1 to 10.
Colour the number 10 and the gloves.

Learn

1	x 10	=	**10**
2	x 10	=	**20**
3	x 10	=	**30**
4	x 10	=	**40**
5	x 10	=	**50**
6	x 10	=	**60**
7	x 10	=	**70**
8	x 10	=	**80**
9	x 10	=	**90**
10	x 10	=	**100**

Count in tens.

10	☐	30	☐	☐
60	☐	80	☐	100

Use the practise panels on these pages to test how well you know the times tables. Write in the answers then look at the tables on the previous pages to check if you are right. Each table has things to colour in.

Practise Panels

1 x 1 =
2 x 1 =
3 x 1 =
4 x 1 =
5 x 1 =
6 x 1 =
7 x 1 =
8 x 1 =
9 x 1 =
10 x 1 =

1 x 2 =
2 x 2 =
3 x 2 =
4 x 2 =
5 x 2 =
6 x 2 =
7 x 2 =
8 x 2 =
9 x 2 =
10 x 2 =

1 x 3 =
2 x 3 =
3 x 3 =
4 x 3 =
5 x 3 =
6 x 3 =
7 x 3 =
8 x 3 =
9 x 3 =
10 x 3 =

1 x 4 =
2 x 4 =
3 x 4 =
4 x 4 =
5 x 4 =
6 x 4 =
7 x 4 =
8 x 4 =
9 x 4 =
10 x 4 =

1 x 5 =
2 x 5 =
3 x 5 =
4 x 5 =
5 x 5 =
6 x 5 =
7 x 5 =
8 x 5 =
9 x 5 =
10 x 5 =

Practise Panels

1	x 6	=
2	x 6	=
3	x 6	=
4	x 6	=
5	x 6	=
6	x 6	=
7	x 6	=
8	x 6	=
9	x 6	=
10	x 6	=

1	x 7	=
2	x 7	=
3	x 7	=
4	x 7	=
5	x 7	=
6	x 7	=
7	x 7	=
8	x 7	=
9	x 7	=
10	x 7	=

1	x 8	=
2	x 8	=
3	x 8	=
4	x 8	=
5	x 8	=
6	x 8	=
7	x 8	=
8	x 8	=
9	x 8	=
10	x 8	=